The Visiting

Born in Donegal, Frank McGuinness lives in Dublin and is Professor Emeritus in Creative Writing at University Dublin. His plays include *The Factory Girls* (1982), *Baglady* (1985), *Observe the Sons of Ulster Marching Towards the Somme* (1985), *Innocence* (1986), *Carthaginians* (1988), *Mary and Lizzie* (1989), *The Bread Man* (1991), *Someone Who'll Watch Over Me* (1992), *The Bird Sanctuary* (1994), *Mutabilitie* (1997), *Dolly West's Kitchen* (1999), *Gates of Gold* (2002), *Speaking Like Magpies* (2005), *There Came a Gypsy Riding* (2007), *Greta Garbo Came to Donegal* (2010), *The Match Box* (2012) and *The Hanging Gardens* (2013) Among his many widely staged versions are *Rosmersholm* (1987), *Peer Gynt* (1988), *Hedda Gabler* (1994), *A Doll's House* (1997), *The Lady from the Sea* (2008), *Oedipus* (2008), *Helen* (2009), *Ghosts* (2010), *John Gabriel Borkman* (2010), *Damned by Despair* (2012) and *The Dead* (2012).

FRANK McGUINNESS

The Visiting Hour

faber

First published in 2021
by Faber and Faber Limited
74–77 Great Russell Street
London WC1B 3DA

Typeset by Brighton Gray
Printed and bound in the UK by CPI Group (Ltd), Croydon CR0 4YY

A CIP record for this book
is available from the British Library

978-0-571-37140-2

2 4 6 8 10 9 7 5 3 1

For Dinah Wood

The Visiting Hour was filmed at The Gate Theatre, Dublin, and had its world premiere streamed on 22 April 2021.

Father Stephen Rea
Daughter Judith Roddy

Director Caitríona McLaughlin
Set and Costume Designer Katie Davenport
Lighting Designer Paul Keogan
Sound Designer and Composer Tom Lane
Production Manager Jim McConnell
Company Manager Michelle King
Stage Manager Donna Leonard
Head of Costume James McGlynn Seaver
Hair & Make-up Sarah McCann
Sound Engineer Andy Walsh
Lighting Technician Eoin Lennon
Stage Crew Aidan Doheny
Stage Crew Dylan Farrell
Photographer Rich Gilligan

Characters

Father
Daughter

A voice on the tannoy

Setting
A care home and its grounds.
A private room, its window opening onto a garden.
A garden bench.

Time
Now

Place
Here

The care home is clean and well run, its unseen staff efficient, kind, of different nationalities.

Its patients manifest different degrees of forgetfulness.

No one here is entirely incapacitated, but no one will be going home.

This is the period after the complete lockdown.

Visitors are allowed again to call and see relatives but must sit outdoors at a window of the room which the patient occupies.

Father sits in a comfortable chair beside the window dressed in a tuxedo, white frilled shirt, bow tie and pyjama trousers.

He is cleanly shaved, his hair trim.

Daughter sits on a bench in the garden beside the open window.

She wears smart jeans and a brightly coloured shirt and scarf, her sneakers a pricey brand, showing signs of wear.

At times a voice sounds on the tannoy.

Father A charming woman, elegant – that will come as no surprise. Gracious in word and gracious in manner. Charming – yes, she possessed oodles of charm – that's how I would describe –

Silence.

The word I would describe – use to describe –

Silence.

Describe –

Daughter Who?

Father Her. The woman –

Daughter Which woman? Who is it now?

Father You must have seen – you know her.

Daughter Who are you talking about?

Father Katie Boyle.

Father sings from 'K-K-K-Katy' by Geoffrey O'Hara. Silence.

Beautiful Katie.

Daughter Katie Boyle?

Father An elegant lady –

Daughter Very much so.

Father Polite, well spoken –

Daughter And perfectly audible.

Father She must have had the benefit of the best of elocution lessons.

Daughter A delight to listen to.

Father A delight to look at.

Daughter So, you fancied her.

Father Who? Fancied – what are you talking about?

Daughter This Katie Boyle, well spoken –

Father Exceptionally so, yes.

Daughter Elegant, audible –

Father What about her?

Daughter You said she was charming.

Father Katie Boyle?

Daughter That's her, the very one – Katie –

Father Boyle?

Daughter The same one. You brought the name up –

Father Weren't we talking about –

Daughter The Eurovision –

Father The song contest?

Daughter What else? You remembered Katie Boyle.

Father Would she be one of the Boyles lived for years down by the Crescent across the road from the convent school? Great singers they all were, the girls especially, altos if I remember – or maybe soprano? Always won at the Feis Ceoil –

Daughter A mountain of medals –

Father Gold after gold medal but I cannot place a Katie among that connection. Very good looking, clean living family. Was there a Kathleen – a Caitriona? Like a dream to me there would have been, but I've forgotten. Could that be who you're thinking about?

Daughter It's not me thinking –

Father Then why drag the mention of this decent woman without warning into the conversation we're having? There she goes, innocently about her own business, causing no offence, harming nobody and here you are stirring dissent against –

Daughter I'm doing no such thing. You're the one brought up Katie Boyle –

Father I do not know this lady. I cannot place her. I accuse nobody or nothing –

Daughter Who's saying you did? But you claim to have met her –

Father Where?

Daughter I'll let you tell me that.

Father Where would I have met her?

Daughter Wherever it was held that year.

Father The song contest?

Daughter The Eurovision – got it in one, Father.

Father Was it a year I won or lost?

Silence.

Maybe I came second, as usual.

Daughter Pipped at the post.

Father Gracious in defeat, I hope.

Daughter Impeccable behaviour, as always.

Father and Daughter sing from 'Are You Sure? by The Allisons.
Silence.

Do you not remember it?

Father Why would I? We didn't win, did we?

Daughter Not like you to be a bad loser.

Father I'm not, but himself is – the brother. What was it we called ourselves? Slipped my mind. But here's the good one – here's why we might have lost the prize, we weren't brothers at all, and they must have found out –

Daughter That's what riled them, did it?

Father Fit to be tied, the adjudicators. Not pleased – not pleased at all. We were just two young fellows. Just friends –

Daughter Must have got together to carry a tune. Did you pick a name for yourselves?

Father Remind me what it was we did.

Daughter Not like you to forget the name of the band –

Father It wasn't a band. It was a duo – of that I'm certain. That I have not got wrong. Two working chaps. Next thing you know – what's happening to us? We're waltzed off to perform our little ditty in front of millions, carrying the hopes of the nation –

Daughter *Irlande ou le Royaume-Uni?*

Father In those days we had the support of all. And we lost.

Daughter Yes, you lost.

Father Not by much.

Daughter You came second.

Father We lost. Came home beaten, tails between our legs. Empty airport, empty street, empty dance halls where we plied our trade. When you blow your big chance, people forget you.

Daughter But you nearly pulled it off.

Father Yet not quite. She was very kind. Very consoling.

Daughter Katie Boyle?

Father One of the girls from the Crescent. Great singers.

Daughter Soprano and alto – isn't that what you say? Mountains of medals at the Feis, winning all before them, coming down with cups and shields, the prizes tripping them.

Father Great singers.

Daughter Like yourself, Father.

Father I was – when?

Daughter When the occasion demanded.

Father Long ago. Days gone by. What do they call it? Once upon a time.

Daughter Once upon a time.

Father I had a voice. Not a bad one, as voices go. And mine, it went. After a while. A long while you have to admit. My voice. It went.

Daughter Not completely, Father.

Father Soon it will – soon enough.

Daughter We're still surviving.

Father For what?

Silence.
A voice sounds loudly on the tannoy.

Voice All visitors are asked to respect the visiting hour, and not to exceed sixty minutes with your loved ones.

Silence.

Father Where am I?

The voice sounds again on the tannoy.

Voice All visitors are asked to respect the visiting hour, and not to exceed sixty minutes with your loved ones.

Father Where are you?

Silence.

Why do you perch yourself sitting outside? Why will they not let you come in? Have you done something?

Daughter What would I have done? Robbed a bank?

Father Taken what was not yours to take?

Daughter I hardly think so.

Father Not the way you were reared.

Daughter You reared me – you remember that much.

Father Of course I remember. Why would I not?

Daughter You tell me – tell me, please.

Father How did you get here?

Daughter I drove, Father.

Father Did you come on the bus?

Daughter No, I drove – in my car, the red car.

Father Were there many on the bus? Did you sit beside anyone?

Daughter The red car – the one you told me to buy. Red's a lucky colour –

Father The robin redbreast. The red kite. A hawk. These days, watch yourself, watch others like a hawk –

Daughter Like a hawk – soar, like a hawk – soaring –

Father Watch yourself.

Daughter Soar to the moon – the stars – to the sun.

Father It gets in your eyes, the sun, if you look straight at it.

Daughter Looking into the sun.

Father Were there many on the bus?

Daughter You as well. Watch yourself. But for what? Can you tell me that?

Silence.

Has the cat got your tongue? Do you still like cats?

Silence.

Did you ever like them?

Silence.

Not going to say anything? Who am I again? Can you tell me? Am I talking into the wind?

Father The moon and the stars and the sun.

Daughter Who am I?

Silence.

The only daughter. The only child. The one who trudges out on her own here, just to see you. Would you prefer if there had been others? Sons – daughters-in-law, grandchildren, my sisters, my brothers, never born – only me. The one girl, just the one girl, that is it, isn't it, Father? Not spoilt though – always giving, never missing a visit. Do you miss me? The rest of the week, when I'm not here, do you miss me?

Silence.

Do I miss you? Me?

Father I cannot place you – are you your sister?

Daughter I have none – there is no sister.

Father She got the red hair from her mother's side. Only her.

Daughter There's no red hair –

Father Does she live in a grand house? Has she, as they say, has she married well?

Daughter She never married – never bought a fine mansion – she was never born.

Father And yet I remember her, clear as daylight. But I'm told by reliable sources she's grown swanky, very much so. She's never here. Never comes to see me. Will she ever come back, do you think?

Daughter How can she ever come back when she's never drawn breath? Never existed. She does not exist. So, let this settle that. Only we two each see the other, I see you, once a week.

Father Have you taken leave of your senses?

Daughter Chance would be a fine thing – how have I taken leave –

Father Once a week you say you see me. Fuck that for a game of cowboys.

Father starts shooting an imaginary gun.

Bang – bang – bang – bang – bang.

Daughter returns imaginary fire.

Daughter Bang – bang – bang – bang – bang.

Father You got me this time.

Daughter I never miss.

Father And you're never out of my sight. I'm poisoned looking at you. Poisoned choking on the lemon drizzle cake you make me eat.

Daughter You say you enjoy it – you ask me to bring it.

Father I enjoy many things. Loads of things. Turkey legs. Soft peaches in the summer with the blush on them. A close shave at my barbers. But I never get that, do I?

Daughter Poor you, so what do you get?

Father You – all I get is you – you.

Daughter Many's a one would be grateful.

Father I'm not.

Daughter I've noticed.

Father I don't know what to do with you.

Daughter Have me put down. Shot in a bag. Bang – bang.

Father You do that to cats.

Daughter You don't like cats.

Father Never could imagine touching a gun.

Daughter Set me alight. Put a match to me.

Father You're a dangerous customer. You need watching.
Are you still jealous?

Daughter Jealous? Why would I be –

Father Jealous? Of me?

Daughter You?

Father Rife with jealousy. Rotten with it. Yellow. Jealous of
her. Your mother.

Daughter What brings her back into your head?

Father Myself and herself, we'd take on the world. Take
them on – take them all on. Beat them blue. Beat the living
daylights – beat the lining out of them. We could leave them
crying. You – you were crying – was it because of me? Did I
hit you?

Daughter No, never laid a finger on me.

Father So, why the blubbering?

Daughter We'd lost her, my mother. We were holding each
other – me in your arms. Tears tripping us.

Father Not me. Not tears from these eyes. Not mine.

Daughter You were drowning in them. Why deny it?

Father These days it's tears wherever you look. Women, children, even grown men, bawling, whinging, over the slightest thing. No backbone. No facing up to the rough into the smooth. All hiding in corners, wiping tears –

Daughter You claim you don't –

Father I can take it, that's the difference. Throw what you like at me. I'll confound it all. I can take a beating. Black and blue.

Daughter Who was it beat you?

Father The bastard from Luxembourg.

Daughter The Eurovision. He swung it.

Father He left us high and dry.

Daughter Whoever heard tell of Luxembourg?

Father You think we should have knocked them into a dark corner.

Daughter It's about the size of a Woolworths store.

Father That's all. And that's who beat us – who beat me, and my brother –

Daughter You have no brother. You know that yourself.

Father Are you telling me I don't know my own brother?

Daughter You don't know your own daughter.

Silence.

Do you know who I am?

Father Why am I dolled up like this? Why the frilly shirt? What's with the bow tie?

Daughter Do you recognise me?

Father You have the look of someone from long ago. Someone long passed away. Gone to meet their maker and receive their reward. Is that why I'm wearing this black jacket? Have I just come back from a funeral? Then why are my trousers like what you'd see on a clown?

Daughter They're pyjamas – your pyjama bottoms.

Father You only put them on at night. This is the middle of the day. Where have they taken my ordinary clothes? Who has nicked them? When will I get them back? Can I go home then? Is that why you've come here? Are you to bring me back to my own house? Speak up. Are you? Speak – speak up –

Daughter Ssh, Father, ssh, ssh.

Father I will not – I will not –

Daughter Ssh, ssh –

Father You're worse than your mother.

Daughter You should not say that.

Father The tight face on the pair of you.

Daughter Lips sealed.

Father She looked down her nose –

Daughter At you and yours. Circus people. Caravans, slot machines –

Father Chairoplanes, swing boats, that's what she thought –

Daughter You were not circus people though.

Father Were we not? I was double jointed, the dashing young man on the trapeze –

Father sings.

'He flies through the air with the greatest of ease,
That dashing young man –'

Daughter You took sick standing on a chair to change a light bulb. That's how good a head for heights you had. And you could barely genuflect.

Father I would bend the knee to no man.

Daughter Wearing a clown's trousers –

Father We were never circus people. I was a singer, a professional entertainer –

Daughter With your brother – your imaginary brother – at the Eurovision, meeting Katie Boyle, beaten by Luxembourg.

Father Where?

Daughter Luxembourg.

Father Never heard tell of it. Never played them in my life.

Daughter Played what?

Father Rugby.

Daughter You never watched a whole match through in your life.

Father I'm agreed with you one hundred per cent.

Daughter No argument then.

Father About what?

Daughter Name your pleasure. Name your poison. One time –

Father Once upon a time –

Daughter There were arguments about everything.

Father And that made us what?

Silence.

Happy.

Daughter Happy together – happy families – our happy family.

Father Were we?

Daughter A family?

Father I say so.

Daughter I'm glad you do.

Father Can we agree on that?

Daughter I suppose we can.

Father And can we agree in Luxembourg rugby is not a popular game – do you know why?

Daughter Enlighten me what they get up to instead.

Father Practising music, writing songs –

Daughter In French?

Father French, if you don't mind. All that foreign palaver, it goes down well on the continent.

Daughter Which continent? Asia – Africa?

Father That's how they win the contest every year.

Daughter The Americas – Australia – Antarctica.

Father We're stuffed, because the bastards, they're too lazy to learn English –

Daughter Europe – Europe.

Father In Luxembourg they speak every other language but English. It's beyond them, so they never vote for us.

Daughter Not a vote, eh?

Father Not a single vote.

Daughter *Nuls points.* So, we lost?

Father Lost, lost again. Came second. Once again.

Daughter It did not happen, Father.

   Silence.

You never sang in the Eurovision. Nor did your brother, in a duet with you. A dream.

   Silence.

All a dream, Father.

Father All in a dream –

Silence.
Father and Daughter sing from 'Wonderful Dream' by Anne-Marie David.
Silence.

Was that the year I did win?

Daughter Some night – some celebration – I give in, you won.

Father Guess which country I represented?

Daughter Luxembourg.

Father Lovely country.

Daughter Loveliest people.

Father They all speak English. Strange isn't it?

Daughter Passing strange.

Father sings.
Silence.

Father What did we promise?

Daughter Whatever you like, Father.

Father speaks.

Father Lost in a dream.

Silence.

We're falling like leaves in September. Falling like fleas. All the old ones. Are we letting them die? Do we want them to? Do they want to?

Silence.

Not worth living. Not worth keeping them alive. Let them go. Let us go. Will you let me die?

Daughter You know I will not.

Father Did I win singing that one about the dream? What was I called then? Do you remember? The strange thing – the funny thing – what am I trying to say?

Daughter You're on your own there, Father.

Father The funny – the strangest thing – I'm certain I was a girl. Isn't that a rare one? The sharp look on your face – am I detecting –

Daughter A sneer –

Father A sarcastic tone – your mother's daughter –

Daughter Who put up with much –

Father I ask again, am I detecting –

Daughter An air of disbelief? Would those be the words that escape you?

Silence.
Daughter sings.
Silence.

Father Is that not it?

Silence.

Is that not my song?

Daughter No, it's not. It's mine.

Father You tell me that, do you?

Daughter You taught me to sing it. You, without patience – me, blue in the face singing it to your satisfaction – red in the face crying, trying to remember it right.

Father If something is worth doing, do it properly. Anyway, this strikes me as highly dubious. Can I believe this sob story? Are you sure it wasn't me sang –

Daughter For Christ's sake, there's lunacy and there's larceny. Theft, that's what I'd call it. Thieving, if you prefer.

Father Hold on a minute –

Daughter Not on this occasion. You sang that song when you were, God bless the mark, a slip of a girl? If you did, Father, it's daylight robbery. You're stealing my life.

Father A bit exaggerated.

Daughter You're stealing my life. Stop, thief. Stop it. Stop it now. I've put up with plenty these past years. I'm not indulging this latest claim. So stop. Stop taking my life, or what little's left of it.

Father Could you do something for me?

Silence.

Would you leave?

Silence.

Leave.

Daughter Where would you like me to go? Where should I go?

Father Luxembourg. You'll fit in well there. You should come across many of your like.

Daughter And who are my like?

Father Half the population of Luxembourg claims they won the Eurovision.

Daughter Half the population has won it.

Father Not recently. There's been a drought of the champagne flowing and the corks popping. Fewer and fewer winners, but more and more schemers claiming to be who they are not and to have done what they didn't, lying through their teeth, brazen faced –

Daughter And am I that brazen face?

Silence.
The voice sounds on the tannoy.

26

Voice All visitors are asked to respect the visiting hour and not to exceed sixty minutes with their loved ones.

Father Who are you?

Voice All visitors are asked to respect the visiting hour and not to exceed sixty minutes with their loved ones.

Father Do I know you?

Daughter You do – you don't – who can tell? Maybe none of us.

Daughter sits.

Father There you go, sitting down again.

Daughter Do you mind me doing that in your presence?

Father Taking the weight off your high heels?

Daughter I'm wearing trainers.

Father Good, you're relaxed. Now you're not upsetting yourself, nor upsetting me.

Daughter Maybe then I should just call it a day.

Father What?

Daughter Stop, maybe.

Father Stop?

Daughter Calling. Visiting.

Father Visiting – stop? Why?

Daughter Be free of you.

Father Free.

Silence.

Daughter Free of you. Give up – this –

Father This nonsense?

Daughter Nonsense. Thinking I'm doing you any good. Doing myself –

Father Any good.

Daughter Spending time with you.

Father The two of us, together.

Daughter Week after week, now we can meet again, the visiting hour. Nearly meet again, you in there, me out here, listening, talking – think it must be going in, something must be, more than you realise, making sense a good part of the time, or just pretending maybe –

Father You would miss it though.

Silence.

Did you miss it?

Daughter The months we were not let meet. Both of us –

Father If you could not come, you would miss it, if they stopped us. I didn't see you for ages. Isn't that right? Why didn't you come? Did they stop you?

Daughter They did.

Father Was that my fault?

Daughter Nobody's fault, Father.

Silence.

Nobody.

Father Nobody's fault. For nobody's there. Knock-knock. Who's there?

Silence.

Nobody. Nobody who – who is nobody?

Daughter Just nobody. Why are you asking?

Father Knock-knock. Who's there. Isabel. Isabel who? Don't know, she's gone. Might have I been married to her? Don't know. Knock-knock.

Daughter Who's there?

Father Ann. Ann who? Ann Easter bunny. Knock-knock.

Daughter Who's there? Is it Anna? Anna who?

Father Anna nother Easter bunny. Knock-knock. Who's there? Yeti. Yeti who? Yeti nother Easter bunny. Knock-knock. Who's there? Consumption. Consumption who? Consumption be done with these bloody Easter bunnies. They're everywhere. Why are we playing knock-knock at this stage of our lives? Is something wrong with us?

Daughter Something wrong.

Father Something wrong in my head.

Daughter Knock-knock.

Father Who's there?

Daughter Me. I am. That's who.

Father Glad to hear it. Glad to see you. Are you glad to see me?

Daughter Yes.

Father And I you.

Daughter Who am I?

Silence.

Father You used to draw things with a pencil. Or was it a box of crayons? Always with a crayon and piece of paper on the table in front of you, drawing –

Daughter What kind of things?

Father Maps, tracing maps, maps of all the countries in the atlas, every shape, every colour. And animals, drawing animals, birds as well, pink ones –

Daughter Flamingos.

Father Pretty flamingos. House – a pink house with a blue door. Or was ours a blue house with a pink door? A rainbow – you drew one for me once.

Daughter When did I stop?

Silence.

Why did I stop? Drawing? Countries, houses, birds?

Silence.

Did you keep any?

Father Why would I?

Silence.

Why am I not wearing shoes?

Daughter Because you're inside.

Father Why have I no socks on my feet?

Daughter You don't need socks if you're not wearing shoes.

Father Nobody darns socks any more.

Daughter Nobody darns anything.

Father A lost knack, the needle and thread – the darning mushroom –

He imitates sewing with a needle.

In and out, in and out, stitch after stitch, in and out –
I would be a dab hand –

Daughter You never lifted a darning needle in your life –

Father continues to sew.

Father Maybe so, but if I had learned, I would have done the craft proud – as I would have, had I turned my hand to shoemaking.

He stops sewing.

But there was no chance to learn a trade in those days, tailoring or –

Daughter You would not have had the patience to master the skill. Patience was never our virtue.

Father I had patience to teach you to sing –

Daughter So you fondly imagine –

Father I didn't need teaching, me standing at the bottom of the stairs warbling a mournful tune called 'Two Little Orphans' – orphans without shoes. I forget how it goes now.

Daughter That melody's escaped you – a blessing, that at least.

Father Shoes, sandals, brogues, broga – that's a word for, a word for –

Daughter Shoes in another language.

Father A foreign language.

Daughter If that's what you care to call it.

Father What would you call it?

Daughter Gaelic, the Gaelic language.

Father Where do they speak that? In Gaul?

Daughter Yes, in Gaul. In Galicia, in Germany, in Guam, in Gweedore, in Guatemala, in Guadelupe.

Father You telling me you could travel anywhere, speaking Gaelic?

Daughter Travel the globe, speaking –

Father And the world would give you a hundred –

Daughter Thousand welcomes.

Father What's that in Gaelic?

Daughter Céad –

Father Míle –

Daughter Failte.

Father and Daughter sing from 'Dear Old Donegal' by Bing Crosby.

Father The flowers. I'm in my flowers – that's what the mad old one lived four doors down from us – that's what she'd shout, and her ancient as the hills. I want no man near me, keep out, keep off – I'm in my flowers. She believed she was the belle of the ball.

Daughter What became of her?

Father Withered –

Daughter Plucked – faded –

Father Dust. No longer in flower.

Daughter You used to swing me on our garden gate. In and out, in and out – out and in, me, on top of the gate, safe because I was in your arms, my father's big, strong arms.

Father I didn't drop you.

Daughter Of course you didn't –

Father Would I still have been smoking then? Did my cigarette not burn you?

He grows agitated.

Did I burn you when I was smoking?

Daughter Why would you burn me?

Father Badness. An evil spell came over me. Who cast it?

Daughter What's causing this panic?

Father I'm not – not – what is it?

Daughter Panicked?

Father Yes. Panic. Everybody seems to be in that state these days. In here – all hands – everybody in confusion over something or other. Do you know why?

Daughter Has it something to do with giving up the cigarettes? Has that torn everybody's nerves to shreds?

Father Has there been some law passed? Are we all ordered to abandon the fags and booze, or what will they do to us? Shoot us?

Daughter Bang – bang – bang.

Father Stop us singing and dancing? What then would become of us?

Daughter Bang – bang – bang.

Father Are they going to close everything down? Shut us up entirely? Stop us even talking to ourselves? Tape our mouths closed? Would they do that to us? Would we let them? Will you let them?

Silence.

Are you getting back at me?

Daughter For what? What am I to do with you?

Father Put me down. Torture me. Cut off my ears – my tongue. Cut away what makes me a man. Get back at me. Get back for being here with me today. My fault you have to trek to this accursed hole. It was you sent me into this wilderness. And you laughed. I heard you. The grin on your face as you passed sentence. A death sentence, God forgive you.

The voice sounds on the tannoy.

Voice All visitors are asked to respect the visiting hours and not to exceed sixty minutes with your loved ones.

Father God forgive my only son.

Voice All visitors are asked to respect the visiting hours and not to exceed sixty minutes with your loved ones.

Daughter Loved ones – Jesus, that is a rare one, an excellent one. The man can no longer tell if I'm son or daughter, and do you know what?

Father Tell me what.

Daughter I'm not inclined to tell you. Why should I? All will happen is what always happens. What will I get? The worst word in your stomach, against me, against the world, taking on all and sundry, in your rage –

Father Why not? Why not? Isn't it your fault?

Daughter What fault? What was done against you?

Father I was born. Born to die.

Daughter So were we all.

Father If you're not my son, are you my father? You have the look of him. His eyes.

Daughter His eyes, his mouth, his arse, his feet –

Father Why are there shoes on your feet, and not mine? Why cast me out? What good can I do here? What use am I? Who can see or hear me in this kip –

Daughter This midden –

Father This byre –

Daughter And the cost of paying for it drains us dry.

Father What are you trying to do?

Daughter Drains all we've gathered together, what little we made our own, leaving nothing or next to it for me in old age –

Father Then that is a shame – a crying shame –

Daughter Crying.

Father Who is? The house, the home, everyone in it? The townland, the village, the city, the country – crying. Everyone living here, are we going to breathe our last gasp?

Daughter No, not the last gasp, I promise.

Father Who will heed our promise?

Daughter She will –

Father She will save us –

Daughter She always does. My mother.

Silence.

You remember her?

Father I forget –

Daughter It was her got you that shirt with the frills that there's days you cannot be parted from. She bought for you on a big birthday that tuxedo, the fancy jacket. She knew you'd love it the minute you tried it on you. Every chance to wear it you took. You dress yourself in what she gave you. That's how much you remember her. And you cannot forget what she said. What was it she always said? Can you recall her very words?

Father shakes his head.

She said, if you must appear before the multitudes –

Father Multitudes –

Daughter Deck yourself out in a style suitable for performing miracles –

Father Miracles?

Daughter You opened your mouth, Father – miracles happen, sometimes.

Father The sound of her voice –

Daughter The sound of your voices, my mother, my father.

Father My child. My daughter. Breathing. Miraculous – we had to try so hard – and then, there you are. Here you are.

Daughter My mother, your wife, Father.

Father I had a wife.

Daughter I remember you, in love, my father, my mother.

Father Where are we now? Where is she?

Daughter Lost.

Father Gone.

Daughter Vanished. Vamoosed. Off the face of this earth. Wandering about the planets. Saturn. Causing riots on Mercury. Bringing havoc to bear on Neptune. Playing camogie on Jupiter. Hearing the music of the spheres bridging Venus and Mars, conducting the whole galaxy.

Father The woman would rarely venture beyond her garden gate if she had her way. She was like that up to the time she was – was –

Daughter Taken –

Father When?

Daughter A while ago.

Father Where?

Daughter The heavens, as I told you.

Father How did she travel there? She took sick on buses. She did not get on a train until she was in her twenties. Planes scared the shite out of her. She didn't learn to drive until she was forced into doing so. You chat about the heavens – taken there, you tell me. Transported. What does that mean? Me as well, is that how I will pop my clogs?

Daughter You're not wearing clogs. No shoes on your feet, no socks –

Father How was she taken?

Daughter A golden eagle.

Father It took her?

Daughter It descended and stretched out its mighty, cruel claws.

Father Was she eating fish and chips? She had a fondness for smoked cod. Pollack turned her stomach.

Daughter The eagle swooped. Struck dumb she was, unable to shriek, she suddenly thought what charms the breast of the savage beast – or bird, in this instance? Music. So, out of the blue, she began to sing. What? A lament from the long ago? An aria that contained the sufferings of the dispossessed? A yearning of this and every other age for consolation and for peace, something to approximate the still sad music of humanity or something more atavistic –

Father She sang 'The Waxies' Dargle', didn't she?

They laugh together.

Daughter The only tune she could carry from beginning to end.

Daughter sings lowly.

'Said my oul wan to your oul wan
Will we go to the Waxies' Dargle?'

Father sings lowly.

Father
'Said your oul wan to my oul wan
Sure we haven't got a farthing.'

Daughter The eagle opened its claws. It let her fall. She was smashed to smithereens on Mount Olympus.

Father sings lowly.

Father
'What will you have, will you have a pint?'

37

Daughter sings lowly.

Daughter
'I'll have a pint with you, sir.'

They sing in duet.

Together
'And if one of us doesn't order soon,
We'll be thrown out of the boozer.'

Father Was her body ever found? Did we search all the hills of Greece? Or did any of this happen? Are we making it all up?

Daughter What do you think, Father? What does your brain, your addled brain, your dying brain, make of this story? Why do I tell it to you?

Father My brain is dying?

Daughter If I cannot get you to make sense of what's true –

Father My brain's addled?

Daughter Then maybe I can get you to believe what defies description. Can I do that? Is this my way of proving I do not – not yet – give up on you?

Father I'm not sure what point –

Daughter I'm making the point I want something, somehow, to make sense to you –

Father Even if I am past sense?

Silence.

There is no sense to be had any more?

Silence.

Am I on the way out? Is that going to happen this day, this hour? Is that what you're trying to let me know? Trying to tell me?

Daughter sings lowly.

Daughter
'Said my oul wan to your oul wan,
Will we go to the Waxies' Dargle?'

Silence.
They sing in duet.

Together
'And if one of us doesn't order soon,
We'll be thrown out of the boozer.'

Father That's what I'd like sung at my funeral. That fucking song. Your mother adored it. Jesus Christ knows why she sang it to me on her deathbed. And why? You want to know why? Because she was not right in the head, that's why.

Daughter My mother was mad?

Father She was not a bastion of sanity.

Daughter And you were, Father?

Father I was a fine singer. I made a good living for us all. Throw it in my face I was no more than a crooner – a showman whose hour came and went, but nobody wanted for anything. Is that not the case?

Daughter Who am I to contradict you?

The voice sounds on the tannoy.

Voice All visitors are asked to respect the visiting hour, and not to exceed sixty minutes with your loved ones.

Father It was a hard life.

Voice All visitors are asked to respect the visiting hour, and not to exceed sixty minutes with your loved ones.

Daughter There are harder ways to make a living. Fishing for mackerel. Shovelling coal –

Father You never lifted anything heavier than a pair of scissors.

Daughter Father, I'm a teacher.

Father You're a hairdresser.

Daughter I teach geography.

Father You used to trim my flowing locks and shave my beard. It was like losing a ton weight off my head and cheeks. I felt lighter. You never do that now. Are we not allowed –

Daughter No, we're not. To touch.

Father Touch.

   Silence.

Geography.

Daughter That's my subject.

Father If that's so, what's the capital –

   Silence.

Where's the capital –

Daughter Which capital? Capital city –

Father Full of people. Some of them dying. Are all of them? They are in here. That much I can take in. Or am I wrong? Am I seeing things? Or not seeing them. Not seeing people.

Daughter Which people?

Father I cannot tell you that. Cannot tell their names. All their names. They've escaped me. Maybe they have none. At least I cannot say – I cannot remember. But they used to be – they were here – when – when –

   Silence.

What is it I'm asking? What can't I remember?

Daughter I cannot tell you that.

Father I can't tell myself either. But I once knew people – people who lived here. And I do not see them these days. A fellow I talked to – younger than me, what did I talk to him about?

He kicks and heads an imaginary ball, growing distressed.

What is it I'm doing?

Daughter Playing football.

Father That's it. Got it in one. Football. He played for – no, he supported – who is it? I cannot think of the side he cheered for, watching on the television. A bit of sport. Where is he?

Silence.

Why have I not set eyes on him? Have they removed him for his own good? Is he not safe to have around the place? Did he do something? Is he a carrier of something cannot be healed? Have the police nabbed him? Should we say something?

Daughter I will when I'm heading off soon.

Father What do you mean, heading off? Where are you heading to? Are you taking leave of your senses? Anything could happen –

Daughter I will be all right, Father.

Father Many's a woman thought that. Many an innocent walked out her front door, pulling it after her, calling behind her she would be home soon. She never came back. She's still out there, lost somewhere, smashed to pieces, you say on Mount Olympus, but you only have to look around you closer to home, ones who used to live here, old women, old boys, left to fend for themselves in the raw sleet and snow, damned once summer lapsed. Are you going to do that to me?

Daughter I have to hit the road, Father. It's nearly up.

Father What is?

Daughter Visiting time.

Father You're not to leave me.

Daughter I've been here the whole hour.

Father Is that all you can spare for me?

Daughter It's all we're permitted –

Father Who decrees this?

Daughter The care home. Every patient –

Father Who calls me a patient?

Daughter Father, you need nursing. You know that.

Father I know no such thing. How dare you leave me? I was good to you. I have proof of that. Thank Jesus I kept that card. Was it Christmas that you sent it? No, no – it was Father's Day. Wasn't I proud as punch – you called me the world's best daddy. That's what you wrote. Did you not send that to me? Was I the world's best –

Daughter You weren't the worst. Not the worst of fathers. I was not – I am not the worst of children, I show up each week. I make sure they keep you clean and comfortable. Because of me, they know your little wants and needs. Wearing the frilly shirt, donning the tuxedo, just to see me. I bring you lemon drizzle cakes and raspberry biscuits. Sweet stuff may be bad for you, but sugar, will it be the death of you? That's now the least of my worries.

Father They're trying to poison me.

Daughter That's not what will poison you, Father. Something else might.

Father What?

Daughter The very air we breathe. That's the new killer.

Father That's what could top us all these days? Wipe us out completely? What bastard came up with that solution? Is that what happened to your mother? Is something similar happening to us all? Well, if it is, I hope I go before her –

Daughter She's gone, Father.

Father Imagine being landed with a burden like me.

Daughter I can imagine it, yes.

Father She never forgave me – never.

Daughter What did she never forgive?

Father Me – marrying again.

Daughter Did you? Who was it you wed?

Father The Beverley Sisters. All three of them.

Daughter They were a bit before my time, Father.

Father Joy, the eldest, and the twins Teddie and Babs Beverley. The best of girls, but not the happiest of unions.

Daughter One fighting with the other?

Father Certainly not. These ladies knew our business. We absolutely had to tie the knot –

Daughter Had to? You got all the Beverley Sisters up the pole?

Father Show a bit of respect. We had to fulfil a business contract, a commitment we signed up to –

Daughter To do what?

Father Advertise milk stout, Mackeson's milk stout. I would walk nifty as you like from one of the sisters to the next, me saying 'Looks good, tastes good, and by golly they do you good'. Every one of those delicate lassies, they scorned stout. You would not see the likes of them quaffing porter. Quaffing – quaffing – what does it mean?

43

Daughter Drowning.

Father As you sure about that?

Daughter It will come back to you, what it means, quaffing.

Father No, I would not say so. But you tell me you're heading off –

Daughter I am. I have to.

Father Well, mind yourself, on your travels. Heading off to conquer the world. All the countries in the world. I have a daughter who's been to all of them, you know.

Daughter I do.

Father Fair cracked about school. Not like her father was. I had to be tethered to the desk or I'd bolt like the hammers of hell. Mad about geography. She must know the capital city of all the countries in the world.

Daughter That's some going – all of them?

Father Name a country. Ask her the capital. She'll tell you.

As the daughter recites these names of countries and cities, all her weariness, despair, anger, love, isolation and wonder manifest themselves through her litany.

Daughter Finland, Helsinki
Greece, Athens
Malta, Valletta
Switzerland, Berne
Cameroon, Yaoundé
Egypt, Cairo
Australia, Canberra
Bermuda, Hamilton
Peru, Lima
Cambodia, Phnom Penh
Iceland, Reykjavik
New Zealand, Wellington

Spain, Madrid
Madrid – Madrid – Madrid.

Father And Luxembourg?

Daughter Luxembourg City.

Father That's where I won –

Daughter The Eurovision? No, you came second – every time, you came second.

Father Fuck it. Are you certain?

Daughter You told me so.

Father When?

Daughter Today.

Father I have no memory of that.

Daughter I do.

Father That's good.

Daughter I think so as well.

Father You'll ask then –

Daughter Ask?

Father All my pals – where they've disappeared?

Daughter They'll show up again – bad pennies, the lot of them, don't you say that?

Father Why do they ignore me? Why cut me off? Why does nobody see fit to answer me? Have they stopped speaking English?

Daughter Maybe they have, Father.

Father Do you know who I blame for that?

Daughter Would it be Katie Boyle?

Father That's the fucker.

Daughter You always claimed she was a lovely woman.

Father How would I know that?

Daughter An elegant lady.

Father I never met her.

Daughter Most gracious and well spoken.

Father When I said I did, I was just taking a hand at you. I was trying to make her jealous, your mother.

Daughter As a breed we are not inclined – she was not inclined to jealousy.

Father And she used to buy that Camay soap this Boyle woman advertised, she swore by it –

Daughter Did the two ever meet?

Father They did, they shook hands. Katie admired how soft they felt, your mother's hands, and your mother, she said, 'Miss Boyle I have you to thank for that, because –'

Daughter She would only let Camay near her face.

Father Katie Boyle was delighted to hear that. But the funny thing about this whole scenario, your mother's skin, it was rough, rough as a briar. Liars, the whole pack of you, my wife, your mother, the Boyle one, and whoever makes their money manufacturing those pink slabs of soft shite, Camay soap, and if she were standing in front of me, I'd tell that to Miss Katie –

Daughter They say she couldn't even sing.

Father Not a note in her skull. What was she doing presiding over a song contest?

Daughter I'll leave you to ponder on that.

Father Remember to get me a football jersey. I'm tired of this frilly shirt. Who bought it for me? Was it you? Are we related?

The voice sounds on the tannoy.

Voice All visitors are asked to respect the visiting hours and not to exceed sixty minutes with your loved ones.

Father You want to get away now, don't you?

Voice All visitors are asked to respect the visiting hours and not to exceed sixty minutes with your loved ones.

Daughter I'd better do as they order me.

Father You better, but before you depart, one final number –

Daughter Father, you must be exhausted – don't –

Father As I said once to a Beverley Sister –

Father sings from 'Give Me the Moonight' by Frankie Vaughan.
Silence.

Was I any good at all? Any good as a singer?

Silence.

Down the years, I made a living at it. More than most can say.

Daughter I'll see you next week – same time – same place. You want a football jersey?

Silence.

I blow you a kiss.

Silence.

You'll be delighted to see the back of me. Do you want me to tell them you're upset not being able to see your pals? Will I ask them to explain why to you?

Silence.

Would you like me to do that?

Silence.

You were in flying form earlier. Not now. You'll be back in a more chatty mood when next I see you. Yes, you were full of conversation early. Maybe you've had enough for one day. Is that the case?

Silence.

You're tired. Worn out. Sleepy. Will you sleep? Sleep – all right.

She blows him a kiss.

So be it.

She exits, leaving him alone.
He whispers to himself.

Father Tired. Worn. Sleep. All right. Are you all right?

Silence.

So be it.